Colorado Romance
Love Notes and Recipes for Romance
from the award-winning
Highland Haven Creekside Inn

Copyright 2010 by Gail Riley
Highland Haven Creekside Inn
Evergreen, Colorado
www.highlandhaven.com

Designed by Amy Kenney

FIRST EDITION
2010

Highland Haven Press, LLLC
Evergreen, Colorado

Every effort has been made to ascertain the sources of poetry and
prose quoted in this book and to properly credit those sources.

Printed in Mexico by Impresora Donneco,
a subsidiary of R.R. Donnelley, Chicago, Illinois.

ISBN #978-0-615-42666-2

Colorado
ROMANCE

Love Notes and Recipes for Happiness

For Statz

Romance

My husband Tom, "Statz," and I celebrated 35 years of marriage and we still have so much romance in our marriage. Some is born of patience and practice, but most is with ease and affection. My heart can still skip a beat when I see him.
This is 1974, San Francisco.

at the Inn

Romance has made its way into nearly every element of the Highland Haven. It's not just the hand-holding, tender kissing, or love-proclaiming romance that we set the mood for, but the rushing creek, blue sky, singing birds, mountain-high version of nature's own perfect romantic elements. Yes, we "ice the cake of love" at the inn with champagne, fresh flowers, soft music, compelling beds and tubs and much more, but the feeling that comes over our guests as they cross our little bridge, and step into a welcoming and comfortably rich environment, perfect for romance. Now is time for just them to focus all the attention on their love lives.

The reason I am able to write this new book is the fact that I have this great love in my life, since college. The Inn is not only a vessel for our creativity, it is such a natural extension of our romance. The Sweetheart Tree, the Lovers Lane, the Anniversary Heart, and the atmosphere that we have created for guests are natural extensions of our love. Not a gooey, perfect love, but a deep, often challenging one, laced with lots of luck and effort.

You will find in these pages my favorite entries, offered from my guests, as to what "Romance" is to them. I think you will be surprised that they do not follow any stereotype, but instead they offer goose-bumpy honesty and sensible sentimentality.

Find the lined journal pages designed for you to reflect and write down memories of your own personal romance and dreams of your future. Write to remember, so that the people you love may one day find what you have shared - the treasured memories of your love story. My hope is that the children of the couples in these love stories will have a written history of their parents' romance. It's the very best of life.

This book is designed for you to find the romance at home that is found at the Highland Haven. Get inspired for dates, drinks, hikes or dinner and get the kick we all need to get back to what is most important in our lives - romance and love!

With Love,

Gail and Tom

Table of Contents

The Guests... One of the best parts of my job is getting to know our guests, connecting on a personal level with many of them. One morning, I hugged a beautiful young couple who became engaged by the fireplace in their cottage. She told me that the night before he simply said, "Marry me." She jumped up and down, stunned by the ring he slipped on her finger. It was at least a "four table" ring, a measure of how far away by tables that the ring is visible. Another darling young couple had just found out that they were expecting their first child. A third couple was celebrating 7 years of marriage, and yet another couple had known each other since 5th grade; now, 35 years later, they were celebrating their 7th anniversary. Imagine the love in the room. These happy milestones occur daily.

Romance Is... I have just loved collecting the input from my guests as to what romance is to them. These collections, along with the journal entries from the books in the rooms, are really the inspiration for this book. Read these sensitive, honest and heartfelt proclamations of the shapes that romance takes in couples' lives. It is life and love at its very best; what is more important?

The Journals... It is extremely rewarding to learn the love stories from our guests, in person and in the dozens of journals that hold such personal tales about their romance. Reading the honest, goose-bump-causing entries from the last 31 years confirms that there is something magical here. The writings are wonderful, emotional and honest, with profound proclamations of love made to each other.

I am reassured that we are offering something meaningful. One guest recently wrote, "Highland Haven is saving America, one marriage at a time."

In the Details... I have met countless men at the Highland Haven, and I include my husband, who have a flair for romantic ideas, sweet gestures carried out with great effort. At the Inn, it is more often the man who plans their romantic and surprise getaway.

*For Guys...*Try some simple romantic ideas that will help you impress your love without having to go too far out of your way or spending too much money. Bring home flowers for no reason or simply find the time in a hectic day to tell her she looks good. Text, call or email. It just takes seconds, and we love to hear compliments! (This works both ways of course!)

Toast each other before dinner or at your "Cocktail Party for Two." Your words don't need to be professional or written by a famous poet. Your own words from your heart are best. Keep it simple and sincere. Tell her something you love about her and then drink to it.

Kiss her goodbye every morning and when you get home. An inviting warm hug at the start or end of a day is always so very welcome and it sets the tone for what's to come.

"We are all told
that people stay in love because
of chemistry, or because they
remain intrigued with each other,
because of many kindnesses,
because of luck. But part of it has
got to be forgiveness and
gratefulness."

-Ellen Goodman

Romance is...

"Being with the one you love, regardless of the time or place. Romantic places rarely exist; instead a place may lend itself to a romantic mood or help create a special moment provided the romance is brought to test. When you commit to providing every need and want for your partner, romance follows."

Getaway

nothing is better for the both of you

It is always a challenge to carve out time for just you two. Whether it is work, kids, sports, arranging babysitters or money, it is the time that is hard to come by. So when guests stay with us, I do my best to thank them for their efforts. And boy oh boy are we all happy when we do get away. The time to reconnect, whether it is a hike, a long sit by Bear Creek, dinner, enjoying breakfast at the inn or just being alone together is so crucial to our romantic lives. I always appreciate that it is not only healthy for the couples but also for the grandparents, the kiddos, as well the families and friends that help make it possible. Our guests leave refreshed, appreciative and more in love. The truth is that the Highland Haven brings out the romantic in all of us, and no matter if our guests are from one block or a continent away, they feel worlds away. Get away often with the one you love; break the day-in, day-out doldrums and remember why you fell in love.

it's in the DETAILS

Usually it's easier to make a getaway happen when one person surprises the other. Set the wheels in motion by committing to a date, lining up a sitter, planning around an important occasion. Not only will you be a hero, but the benefits are priceless and long-lasting. Ask the innkeeper for any help and remember to route emails and phone confirmations carefully. Shhh, it's a surprise.

From the Journals...

"My wife and I really needed this! We have enjoyed this beautiful room with the cozy fireplace to just take life slow for a precious few moments. Talking while sprawled out across the big bed was a special treat, getting to know each other in new ways after almost 6 years of marriage. We feel like we found ourselves in some respect. We are blessed to live in Colorado, where places like this wait to ease your troubles away."

"The really nice part of living in Colorado is that the escape to a little corner of paradise is so quick! Being able to celebrate our anniversary away from the "usual grind" brought a truly relaxing, fulfilling feeling over both of us."

"This was a surprise get away night for my husband just to say 'I am still crazy about you.' This cottage says that to everyone who has the chance to enjoy it. Romance is only dead to those who have no heart."

"This place allows me to show my wife how much I love her. We both enjoyed the outside world. So if you love your wife as much as I love mine, bring her here with a bottle of wine and some roses and give her the love and time she needs to know just how much she is loved and cared for."

"What a wonderful time! We stayed here on our wedding night 3 1/2 months ago, since then it has been a great adventure getting to know each other. I can't wait to see what the years will bring. This time was also a great time to reminisce; unfortunately, we must be separated for a time as I go to serve my country in the armed forces. With only a few days until my departure this was the perfect time and place to create the memories that will sustain our love over the coming separation. The special spark that grew into flames 3 months ago is still going strong. We can't imagine loving each other more! Just wait 10 years; it will be out of control!"

JOURNALING

Our favorite place to escape to is...

_____

_____

_____

_____

_____

_____

_____

_____

_____

_____

_____

_____

_____

_____

_____

_____

_____

_____

For as long as we can re-member we have had a pair of ducks each summer that sit on our creek in front of the inn. Though they are not always the same couple, I have always given them the names of Herb and Lois. The original Herb and Lois were a lovely couple that were our neighbors in Indiana, where I grew up. They were a lovely, devoted couple-tender with each other.

When they were alive, my mother thought it best not to tell them that I have named water fowl after them. But, all these years later, I believe they would find it dear and romantic to be name sakes for all these devoted pairings of Bear Creek ducks, anguishing in a shady pool in Colorado.

From the Journals...

"The heart knows where it belongs no matter how distance and time keep it afar, there are no forces greater than that of love to bring us back. Together eternal, I shall remain content and hopeful."

✛ ✛ ✛

"The way this place makes us feel is magical, we will always return."

✛ ✛ ✛

"What a break from L.A. No noise, no people, just the beauty of the mountains and my wife."

✛ ✛ ✛

"We came here on the recommendation of a friend of a friend so we came without any expectations. We're leaving with a feeling that some very deep needs were met. A time to make each other feel special and that much necessary connections made again. It's the anniversary of our first date 11 years ago. As I read back the diary of wedding anniversaries up to the 47th anniversary, and everything in between, this "haven" will hold special memories for many, including us. Often it is hard to find the needed special romantic feelings we need, but you've provided a very special place for it to happen."

✛ ✛ ✛

"In this same journal on May 28th I wrote about our visit when Dominic asked me to marry him, now we are married. The most perfect wedding was on March 22, 2008. For a million reasons it could not have been better, but mostly because we are meant to be together. There was so much love in that day; family, friends; and perfect strangers! Needless to say, there was not a dry eye in the room. Thank you Dominic, for choosing me to be your wife. I love you with my heart. So, of course, there was no other place for us to be on our honeymoon than here at the Haven. As usual, everything was perfect. The last surprise I had for my husband was our stone in the Lover's Lane. He so excited and it is beautiful. This has been the most perfect 3 days. What a wonderful way to start our life together!"

"Many seeds sown in the Gardener's Cottage.
Listening to the lilting lyric of the river run;
the whisper of wind
through the spruce's spires, and even the morn's chime of church bells
made hormones to your hearts
as our love bloomed.
Another seed sown here at the Gardener's Cottage"

✛ ✛ ✛

"On October 8, 1987, my husband and I ascended on this wonderful place as "newlyweds."
We were 18 years old and didn't have much money. In '87 the Highland Haven was not so
elegant and luxurious as it is today, but in our eyes it was simply heaven on earth.   Once we
reached our 10 year anniversary, my husband surprised me once again with a wonderful, romatic
night here at the Highland Haven. What's more, is we stayed in the same cabin, Blue Spruce.
The cabin had been updated and was so wonderful. It appeared to have grown and flourished as
our relationship had. Now it is 2007 and we just celebrated our 20th. I feel like I just rolled the
lucky "7's" as we live and love in the wonderful cabin once more!"

✛ ✛ ✛

"My wonderful husband and I are here celebrating 17
years of marriage. He is 75 years old, I am 56. For
those of you reading who may struggle with you love -
please rememer that "love" is the answer to all your
problems. Age doesn't matter, money, time, nothing. It
is all irrelevant if you have long given love freely and feel
loved. Love gives us strength and courage to handle any
of life's problems. If you are young reading this, please
take heed, because life is so short and before you know
it, it is gone. God has blessed us with more time. My
husband was not supposed to live until Christmas of '06
and here it is a year and half later. we have learned so
much on this "borrowed time." We have learned to live
life now - don't wait until you retire because tomorrow
might not come. Another life lesson learned was one of
kindness. To be kind does not take money or time. It
can be a simple hug or a smile. I love my husband so
much. Say a prayer."

Blue skies
Smiling at me
Nothing but blue skies
Do I see.

- Irving Berlin

Proposals
on bended knee

So you've been dwelling over it for months and the time has come. The way you ask a woman to marry you can be a story that is cherished by your wife for a lifetime or it can live in infamy forever. Ask your trustworthy friend, her family member or your innkeeper! to assist you in accomplishing your plan. For those a little nervous about the moment of truth, here are the basics and a few samples to put your mind at ease.

it's in the DETAILS

Buy the biggest bouquet of flowers ever! Red Roses are appropriate but keep in mind her favorites-not all women love red roses. Pink? Does she prefer peonies or tulips? Go to a florist and get at least a dozen.

Make a statement by having rose petals strewn on the bed and perfectly chilled champagne ready to pop!

Yes, you should get down on one knee. This tradition is heart-melting for her. Tell her in your own way that she is the most beautiful woman in the world, and you would be honored to have her hand in marriage. Talk about your future. It is brilliant.

From the Journals...

Him: "This place really does feel magical. I love the stream being right outside the cabin. I loved it so much that it became the inspiration to ask the woman I love more than life to be my wife. The chairs by the creek made a perfect cuddling and preparing spot. It was almost as beautiful and perfect as my new fiancée. Oh, and she said "yes!" **Her:** "Last night the sweetest, kindest, most loving man I have ever met asked me to spend my life with him. Although I would have said "yes" no matter where he asked me, this place made the perfect setting!"

"Okay, so this was so not expected! My boyfriend decides that we are running away for a night and here we are! This was the perfect setting, a cozy cottage, a small fire, and poem from my love and he was on his knees. The question I have waited a lifetime to be asked and I said, "Yes!" We will definitely be back for more! This was the best weekend of my life. And one I will never forget. Oh god, how do I tell my mom? Tomorrow is April Fools!"

"The love we found in this room was so overwhelming and strong that we didn't feel we should take it all with us so we left some here for the next pair of lovers who weren't sure what they would find here. They can take some of the love but they must leave some behind for the next pair of lovers as well. We left enough behind for everyone to share and enough to last as long as this cottage shall stand."

"Two years ago my husband proposed to me in this room. We've decided that it was so magical and romantic that we will come back every year on our engagement anniversary. Last year we returned as newlyweds. This year we returned with our 3 1/2 month old son. The magic remains."

"Let me just say I can honestly not speak clearly right now...this is how happy and excited I am. I just got engaged at Evergreen Lake to the love of my life - my best friend. I'm so blessed and very much loved. He has done nothing less than everything. He's my angel, my protector, my rock, my everything."

15

JOURNALING

Our storybook tale...

_____

_____

_____

_____

_____

_____

_____

_____

_____

_____

_____

_____

_____

_____

_____

_____

_____

_____

_____

_____

From the Journals...

"What a perfect and magical ending to a perfect and magical day!
Yesterday Ben and I were married in the Rocky Mountains in a very small but special ceremony. We had the bluest and clearest skies that only Colorado can produce..."

"Spring brings about more than beautiful flowers! Each and every day I ponder and search for special ways, places and things to show and do for the woman I love so dearly. What a special place you provide for people in love. I came to your Haven to propose to a very special "lady," to have and keep my name forever and a day. Of all the beautiful places we've encountered this is a little piece of heaven. (She said yes!) Thank you from both of us and our hearts for an unfathomable memory for us to cherish always."

Just Married

Sometimes she has her hair still half up, a little leftover glitter, a beautiful French tip manicure suitable for the exquisite diamond, now next to a wedding band. He figits with his band - it may be a long time until it is comfortable.

Mostly, the "husband" and "wife" have a glow, a relaxed just-out-of-bed comfort mixed with relief that the wedding has passed and they are now married. The first time we talk at breakfast I am sure to use the words "husband" and "wife," to their delight.

Nothing is lovelier than these couples, radiantly happy. And there is no part of my job I enjoy more.

it's in the DETAILS

I couldn't have said it any better...

"Loving your soul mate with all of your mind, body and soul. Taking the time of our life to remind each other that there would be no life without the other."

From the Journals...

"Our first anniversary. All the planning was done by my husband, so when we arrived I wasn't sure what to expect. When we pulled in it was a moment of tranquility. The creek reflecting the afternoon sun seems to dance. Our room reflected romance in each articulate detail; and invited you in to relax, surrounding you with fresh air to breathe in and rejuvenate."

Lovers Lane

Years ago we re-designed the path leading from our main lodge to the creek through the 80-foot blue spruce trees. I admire walkways that have some significance: pavers that have names for tender re-membrances or that were sold and placed to raise funds for worthy causes.

Our Lovers Lane now is home to dozens of stepping stones that have been personalized with carved lovers', girlfriends', even childrens' initials. They are scattered under the trees. Often, they are a surprise for him or her, ordered in advance of their stay. We can see couples stroll to the path where they pause over their own stone and embrace at the surprise. It is pretty sweet.

it's in the DETAILS

I wanted my stones to be simple carvings - like engravings of initials marking love, "setting it in stone." Ask your local sign maker or engraver if they could do one for you. It is a uniquely thoughtful and lasting gift for the one you love or a sensitive wedding or anniversary gift!

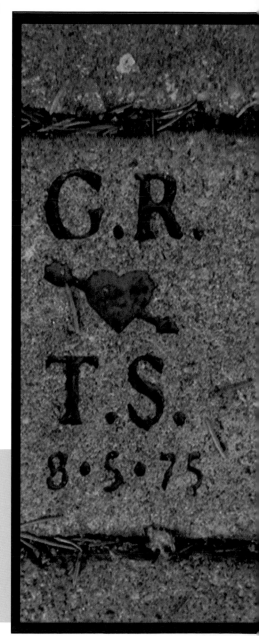

From the Journals...

"Greg and I were married at the Evergreen Lake House today! The setting was perfect, now a full moon, a beautiful delicate snow, surrounded by the people we enjoy most. What made it even more spectacular was coming home to Highland Haven and coming back to a crackling fire. We will forever hold this memory."

"After two night in the Fireside Loft we are the two happiest people on earth, well it might be because we got married last night! Thank you for a perfect place to stay on our perfect wedding weekend. We will see you on our first anniversary!"

"Well just as I predicted on 4/2/01 we came back for our wedding night!"

Jenny and I got married here at the Highland Haven tonight. It was beautiful with our family down by the creek with the bag-pipes playing in the background."

"What a perfect way to spend the first day of the rest of our life together. This place is almost as beautiful as the woman I married. Still hard to believe that she said yes. As I write this I am as emotional as I was when we exchanged our vows. These last few days are ones a person never forgets."

"We had a magical time. Our son and daughter gave us this wonderful anniversary present. This is the room in which our son proposed to our terrific daughter-in-law. They couldn't say enough about their experience. And now, neither can we."

JOURNALING

How we felt on our wedding day...

Tyler ❤ Alisha
2.29.08

Steve ❤ Rebecca
9·12·08

Gail ❤ Chuck
5·7·05

Dale ❤ Tina
8·01·08

Analicia & Nana BFF

Stepping

Mike and Carla Inamorati

Inamorati is plural for Inamorato: In love, fond of, crazy about, in love with.

Sarah ❤ Sean
8·09·08

Krisinda ❤ Andrew
5.17.08

Marlo ❤ Ian
7·8·00

MIKE ❤ CARLA INAMORATI

John ❤ Marla
5·2·09

Jared ❤ Heather
6·20·03

Marlo and Ian were married on the grounds of Highland Haven and celebrated their 10th anniversary here again in 2010!

S.D. 40TH
6·9·08

Jon ❤ Amy FOREVER

Becks ❤ Brock
9.30.06

27

Zach ♥ Meagan 5·11·08

Sandra ♥ Domonic 3-22-08

Emily ♥ Michele 11·19·05

Emily and Michele stay every November 19th to celebrate their anniversary. They book their room 1 year in advance

Stones

Sue ♥ Sid 2-14-04

Jackie ♥ Chuck FOREVER

B.A. ♥ R.S. 9·2·2000

Having stayed at the Highland Haven 12 times, here they mark their 52nd anniversary and a second stone was made to take home.

Tracy ♥ Carolyn 3·13·99

Tommy ♥ Joanne 7.30.05

Dustin ♥ Lisa 6·27·99

Ben ♥ Wendy 3·5·08

Amy ♥ Jeffrey 9·12·09

Scott ♥ Jenny 10·19·07

Alexandria ♥ Burt 52nd Jan 28, 1956

My Sweetheart

On our 34th anniversary Tom took me to breakfast and surprised me with a rusted steel heart that our local welder hand made from his design. It has our initials, T + G, carved out surrounded by cross hatch counting, adding up to 34. I just love it and have made them available to our guests celebrating their anniversaries as well. Mine hangs from the arbor outside our house and I see it daily.

Sweetheart Tree

couples testaments of love

At the Inn we had a huge tree fall on the main lodge the year we bought it. It was hard to shake the possibility that it was "a sign" that we just might have made a mistake, in the debt and challenge we had just gotten ourselves into. We took the mess and expense it cost us and turned it into something special. We left almost 15 feet of the stump and had the idea to save it for carvings of initials of our guests who celebrated their love here and wanted to "leave their mark." There in the tree, deeply carved hearts are filled with initials of guests. I tried to make a living as a wood carver in the 1970s, and my carving tools are now loaned to any guest who wants to use them on the tree. Stripped of its bark, the tree has offered memory space to uncounted couples who have visited the inn, many to return again and again. The Sweetheart Tree was soon full. We now have added a second Sweetheart Tree gradually filling with new lovers' initials and names. I don't have to imagine the lovers here; I get to meet them and be small part of their romance.

My love of trees and the woods has never waned.

it's in the D E T A I L S

It is not so much for its beauty that the forest makes a claim upon men's hearts, as for that subtle something, that quality of air that emanates from old trees, that so wonderfully changes and renews a weary spirit.
- Robert Louis Stevenson

"I'm grateful to my father who had our names carved in the bear tree...it makes this place even more special and memorable. It's so hard to leave, but...we'll be back."

33

34

Spring

Springtime in the I

ockies is Romance

Over the last two years we have collected the thoughts and written accounts of what "Romance is" to the guests of Highland Haven. Here is the collection.

Romance is...

"...being in a cozy mountain inn relaxing and chilling out and just talking about a wonderful busy day and then getting totally dressed up for a wonderful dinner. Romance is simply just being with the person you love and adore...even if you are at home watching the ducks on the pond whilst you sip a lovely glass of wine and grill and prep your own dinner. It is just so important to be with the person you love most in this world...safe and cozy and protected."

♥

"...You can tell when you are in love when you can enjoy doing things with that special someone when ordinarily under differing circumstances you would not want to do it at all."

♥

"...achieved when love, strength and friendship endures through arguments, heartache and adversity. When one has the ability to look back over time loving and accepting the other in spite of spiritual, physical and intellectual change then they are rewarded with romance: a fireplace, bottle of wine and passionate sex that knows no age."

♥

"...getting stuck for 7 hours in the snow, finally getting to your room and finding it has no power and not wanting to do it any other way."

♥

"...that special, unplanned moment when you look at partner and think, "I am still madly in love!"

♥

"...marrying your fifth grade sweetheart 35 years later then 42 years later he brings you on a surprise ro-night to just 'breathe' together."

Romance is...

"...coming to the most romantic bed and breakfast in Denver for my best friends wedding and getting proposed to."

♥

"...spending our 15th anniversary in such an incredibly romantic haven just makes us realize how much we are both inspired by beauty and nature and that we picked the right people to go through life together. Thanks for the beautiful memories."

♥

"...a crisp sunny day in the mountains, hand in hand."

♥

"...closeness, time spent with no distractions. Talking and dreaming with my husband and touch with intimacy and sex. Romance is the atmosphere produced under varied and special circumstances- times when we cherish our special circumstances- times when we cherish our spouses...an intimate connection through the spirit level. We believe romance connects our deep emotions to the physical expressions of love."

♥

"...Ken, my husband. He planned this 5-day trip for months. I didn't know where we were going or what we would be doing. He ordered flowers for our magical room. Horseback riding, his and hers massages. On the day of our 25th anniversary he hired a photographer to take pictures as he got down on bended knee and gave me a 3-carat diamond."

♥

"...to know how to be in love in silence."

Romance is...

"...the delight in sharing. Be it your innermost secrets, a casual touch, a playful look or a sensual exchange. Sharing your everyday moments is what makes them memorable and real. And seeing your joy reflected in your partner's eyes is what makes them romantic."

♥

"...the small things that add up over time through the rhythm of meaningful repetition. Examples: fresh flowers, holding hands, sharing memories, inside jokes, long days in the sun, the ocean, staying in $20/night accommodations in remote locations around the world, morning kisses and, of course, waffles at the Highland Haven."

♥

"...the desire to do whatever it takes to make your loved one happy. Doing all the small things that show your appreciation."

♥

"...always holding that special look, that special smile, that special squeeze, that special place in your heart and mind and soul where you can retreat with your own princess or prince to escape from the tedium and demands of everyday life. (We have been to many romantic places during our 40 years of married life and Highland Haven ranks very near the top of the list!)"

♥

"...when you love someone unconditionally. All efforts are made to be a lover, partner, and friend. Romance can be as simple as a smile, a kiss and gleam into each other's eyes. Spontaneity is great. Go to a private place to be alone. Hold each other to hear heartbeats, make love, whisper and sing sweet nothings. Making each other feel special and loved and give space to a person and be an anchor for each other."

♥

"...never wanting to let go, wanting to sit in the same chair with each other, serving each other and sharing coffee."

42

Romance is...

"...love, the kind of love that makes your heart skip a beat and gives you butterflies in your stomach. Romance is friendship, sharing laughs and talking for hours about random topics. Most important, romance is two people each bringing their own differences and unique qualities and joining them together to create a great love and friendship in their heart, mind and soul."

♥

"...being able to enjoy every day because you know the person you're with will be with you forever."

♥

"...is a cozy fireplace, sound of a rushing creek, smell of pine trees and flowers, birds singing, relaxing with the one you love at the Highland Haven."

♥

"...knowing that the man I spend each night with is the man I vowed to spend each night with. He loves me desperately and unconditionally. I never have to wonder if he'll call or if I'll see him again. Our love is pure and unadulterated."

♥

"...is found in abundance when we take our focus off what we deserve and look at ways to serve."

♥

"...riding the white water together in health and harmony. Later, enjoying a bottle of organic wine next to the creek (at Highland Haven) talking about inspiration and evolution of thought. The morning after, sharing a lovingly made breakfast over a conversation about human rights with Gail."

♥

"...a comfort and a thrill steadfast and ephemeral."

This is the same nest in the same tree just two weeks later. Spring just explodes at last!

Springtime in Colorado, and especially at our altitude of 7000 feet, is full of anticipation! Most years it just takes it's sweet time. We can - and usually do - have a surprise snowstorm in May, right after we finally put away our boots and coats. But, when spring comes, it comes with all its glory. The freshest brightest shades of green, the warbling birds and our rushing Bear Creek make us forget all about winter. We just love it!

Typically, we then jump right into summer and we are off to take in the magnificence of a Colorado summer. Now starts the fun flurry of music and art fairs, farmers' markets, picnics, biking and hikes with our dogs. And of course, love is in the air! The inn is bursting with couples celebrating, proposals and weddings.

Romance is...

"...The word 'romance', to some people, implies something fleeting. Something with a beginning, a middle and an end. It can't possibly last, right? Boy, is that ever depressing. Fortunately, it can also imply an ongoing, emotionally deep attachment between two people. One that lasts and weathers both the fair and the stormy throughout time."

♥

"...two people, together for many years, can make many habits in their relationship. Some good, some bad. Romance is the effort it takes in a relationship to transform the ordinary into the extraordinary. Striving to bring the good habits to the surface, but with flair. Romance is listening to your beloved's heart, to the words they say as well as the ones they don't, and show them you hear them. Be creative. Be open. Be serious. Be silly. Be loved."

♥

"...more than a physical expression of affection, it is the outworking of love by means of deep commitment, and selfless service to one another, seeking creativity and spontaneity oh, and a weekend at the Highland Haven doesn't hurt!"

♥

"...warmly and slowly melting together day after day and looking forward to the next."

♥

"...Jim and Kay were going to marry Sept 9, 1959. Kay called the wedding off 3 days before and they both went their separate ways. It has been 50 years and their spouses have passed away. Jim and Kay have re-connected and will marry Aug. 29, 2009. To God be the Glory."

♥

"...selling your car, quitting your job, and condensing your things to fit in a single backpack to travel across the country bouldering and canoeing with the man you love when both those things scare you. But it is all worth it, every moment of it, when you wake up every morning, whether dirty in a buggy tent or fresh in a beautiful suite he bought for you and he tells you every morning that you are gorgeous and he loves you. I love you too."

Romance is...

"...looking into your partner's eyes and seeing that sparkle that says, "this is where you belong.""

♥

"...when you are in the middle of a chore, dressed in your "grubbies" sweaty and dirty and you realize that your lover is watching you with passion in their eyes - it's so romantic!"

♥

"...a walk in a snowfall, books by the fire, a dance in the rain, a new adventure, coffee in bed, and a walk on the beach, star gazing with my sweetie."

♥

"...always knowing you are loved, no matter what."

♥

"...communicating on many levels with the one you love - no matter where you are."

♥

"...working hard for a year with the knowledge that, with what you save, you can spend more time together than you have before. We are rock climbing our way across the country with no specific plan or direction."

♥

"...getting away from the business of everyday life with the one you love and realizing that your life, spouse, kids and faith is everything you could have asked God for."

♥

"...is the never-ending excitement of anticipation the arrival of the love of your life, be it the end of a long day at work or the return from a business trip."

Romance is...

"...a deep, tender and unselfishness between two people that draws the hearts warm to the surface in and outward display of love and caring."

♥

"...when a single touch or glance speaks a thousand words. Quiet time together is comfortable and safe."

♥

"...your sweet husband riding his bike alongside you as you run 18 miles."

♥

"...waking up each and every day with the one you love and retiring in the evening in each other's arms thanking the Lord for another beautiful day. What happens between those hours is a gift."

♥

"...remembering why you fell in love in the first place no matter how long you have been together. It is candlelight dinners with massages to follow preferably in a hideaway you both adore."

♥

"...the process of making your love feel cherished! The moment when he catches me off guard in an unexpected moment and says, "Gosh, I love you!""

♥

"...living beyond the everyday pleasures with each other...the loving, the laughing, the understanding, the forgiveness!"

51

 Romance is...

"...the anticipation of "what's next" with the wonderful person chosen as a friend, partner and lover."

♥

"...the excitement of each new surprise planned for us to share...whether it's a stay along the California coast in Cambria & Pismo Beach, or in Solvang and dinner at the famous Hitching Post II in Buelton."

♥

"...a Colorado get-a-way whether to the Brown Palace, The Boulderado, the Golden Hotel, or to the wonderfully romantic Highland Haven Creekside Inn in Evergreen."

♥

"...telling that special person when we are apart, their arms are always around each other."

♥

"...when your first name becomes "gorgeous"... love notes packed in a snack bag every morning... fresh flowers when he sees last week's bouquet begin to fade...knowing you are loved and adored the way you have always dreamed of."

♥

"...togetherness without interruption or agenda, with a little 'splurge' thrown in for good measure."

♥

"...a double standard. Whereby you accept things from each other that you would not from another person."

♥

"...the tender touch of beseeching promise, the soulful gaze sans artifice, and a vision that lifts two spirits in spiraled exaltation."

Romance is...

"...I am beginning to feel that all I dreamed about is alive and walks and talks. No other would ever do."

♥

"...spending time alone with the one you love, doing the things you both enjoy. Hands clasping, glances meeting, that special bond that never fails. "

♥

"...loving and being loved through time and distance and even after years of separation being at the same place you left off...connected in mind and body and soul. Romancing your love after 30 years of hopeful dreams and then living today with a heart full of love and hope to be shared together forever."

♥

"...not to be confused with love which has many forms. Romance is an expression of one form of love which helps bind two people together, often for a lifetime."

♥

"...when we can detach from your children for 24 hours to a place that is serene and quiet; where we can finally look into each others' eyes and bond once more. We love coming to High-land
Haven for the quick little snippets of reconnection. "

♥

"...taking time to reflect on life to determine what is true in your heart and then acting on that regardless of who it is with; yourself, significant other, family or friends!"

♥

"...the little touches, the details that say "I care about you and I took the time to think of what you would like, not me." It is also having someone to share your life with; the ups and downs, the trials and tribulations. "

Romance is...

"...waking up next to the love of your life, beside a creek in the Colorado mountains."

♥

"...to just pack up everything and leave your old life behind when your spouse suffers from homesickness. My husband (then boyfriend) did so 15 years ago to move to my native Germany- and he loves it there. Can't think of anything more romantic."

♥

"...looking into your wife's eyes and praying that every moment I am blessed with her in my life, I can bring a smile to her face."

♥

"...revisiting a beaver damn we found on our honeymoon in 1975. We watch the come out to swim and they in return watch us. Each year we take photos of our ourselves a the same boulder, marking each year of love."

♥

"... for us it's "date night" when we cook together. We alternate serving as chef and sous-chef. Like W.C. Fields, "we always cook with wine and sometimes we even put some in the food.""

♥

"... the time we spend present in our love. It is when we put aside distractions and think, feel, and act from the heart. It can be something as simple as holding hands at the right time; or something as elaborate as a champagne dinner on a mountain peak. What is important is the genuine, natural expression of love."

♥

"...staying married for 27 years, still being in love and blessing our children in marriage. Romance is rekindling your love and staying at the Highland Haven. "

Ice Vodka Sculpture

♥ Place your tall bottle of vodka, gin, schnapps or any liquor that is delicious icy cold into a 2 quart milk or OJ carton. (paper, not plastic)

♥ Center and fill to the top with water.

♥ At this point you can place flowers, branches, berries around the sides in the water.

♥ Place upright in your freezer. (Or outside to freeze if cold enough)

♥ Peel the carton away to reveal your "ice sculpture."

♥ Place in a decorative shallow bowl, dish or plate.

♥ Tie on a pretty napkin for pouring.

♥ Pour into your favorite glasses and enjoy!

Summer

Here's to us!

Cheers!

Cocktail Party for 2

a toast to love

Sometimes a "Cocktail Party for Two" at home is better than heading out with a group or to a party. Have your own cocktail party for just you two and make it memorable. Dress up a little, set the mood with your favorite music and pick a special spot; on your deck by summer, in the winter by the fire, or in the bedroom! Pull out your best glasses or buy new ones – they can be inexpensive but make the drinks taste even better. (I have a big collection of pretty glasses – drinks do taste better in a good stemware.)

Dedicate a toast to you two. Celebrations are the best and you just can't have too many of them.

it's in the DETAILS

We all have our favorites and I offer here the classics with a twist. For summer cocktail pleasure, few drinks can rival the bright, citrusy Gin and Tonic. I like Bombay Sapphire.
Vodka is just as good if you prefer.
Here the tonic water ice cubes make the difference!

Picnic for Two

get close to nature and get close to each other

Everyone has a special or favorite spot for a picnic: under a shady tree, in the park or woods, even in your own back yard. You can make it as involved or simple as you like.

Just being out of doors makes the food taste so very much better! Here in Colorado we can hike a mountain, find a stream, or find shelter under a huge pine tree. Throw down a blanket, get comfy and marvel at the scenery and at being together. Nature brings out the best in all of us: healthy exercise in the hike to find the perfect spot along with slowed down time for conversation.

it's in the D E T A I L S

The best part of a picnic is the quality time it provides. Be sure to leave your cell phones in the car so you can just talk to each other and enjoy each other's company. Take your cameras and do a "self timed" portrait. Have it printed and framed. Don't just leave it on your computer!

I have laid aside business and gone a fishin'

Fly Fishing

he'll love you for it

Fly fishing is the perfect blend of nature and romance. It is a "couples-pleaser" to enjoy a sport that is so very satisfying and potentially, very exciting – for both of you. Truly, what could be more fun than standing in a beautiful creek in waders up to your hips casting into beautiful pools of water anticipating a rainbow or brown trout on your line? Actually catching one has never been that critical to me because just being in that kind of beauty is magic to me. Keep your picnic menu simple. Remember that you or your sweetie could be carrying your lunch quite a ways to find the perfect stretch of the Colorado creek or mountain lake. Pull out the Tupperware and stick to basic good food. We love these Mini Basil Sandwiches. Remember to bring your favorite novel for a good read on the shady banks.

it's in the D E T A I L S

...healthy. Try a batch of our healthful Mountain Energy Bars to energize you for your hike. Add Colorado Micro-Brews or fill some water bottles with Lemonade or iced tea. You're set!

Date at Farmer's Market

plan your dinner with fresh ingredients.

Statz and I go to our local farmer's market and have such a great time. I get overly excited about fruits, vegetables and flowers and he loves the deliciously fresh and unique food served up on the spot! "Shopping" at a farmer's market just feels right. Supporting local vendors who offer up their very best home grown and home made goods is healthy for our local economy, our planet, our sense of well-being, and certainly our stomachs! Let the food inspire you. I go right for the tomatoes, hoping that they will be as good as what we grew in my Indiana home. If you like to can, now is the time! I load up on items for the inn; colorful small potatoes, cheeses, veggies for our daily egg stratas, and any and all fruits from our beautiful state. Colorado can not be beat for its corn, melons, beans just to mention a few. Take advantage of your state's unique fresh offerings and prepare as simple and fresh as you can!

it's in the D E T A I L S

Trust your market vendors to help you select their best produce and products. You will find them to be a wealth of knowledge on how to prepare and make use of the fruits of their labor to their very best potential. If you can, buy extra to freeze or share with a friend or neighbor. Fresh fruits and vegetables make wonderful gifts!

Autumn

81

Love

Everything is calmer, quieter in the fall. The change of the season brings the comfort of settling in for the months ahead. In the Colorado mountains the season begs a hike in the woods. Elk sightings are common and the aspens look like flickering gold.

From the journals...

"What a delight to be here with my bride of 15 years. The spirit of this place along with the beauty of the woman I love, made this time so special... a slice of heaven on earth."

. . .

"He showed me a day full of romance, seduction and serenity. We danced by the firelight, and I let my soul soar like never before. Love is a language softly spoken between two hearts."

Sweet Dreams

May your night be filled with the simple pleasures of a starry night, crisp mountain air and the sounds of Bear Creek to lull you to sleep.

83

A Fall Walk

The days are getting shorter and the leaves in Colorado are starting to turn a sparkly gold. It's fall! Some people may hang their boots up until spring, but some of the very best hiking of the year is waiting. There are far fewer people, more wildlife, (elk, deer-hopefully, no bears or mountain lions!) and I challenge that there are few states more beautiful than Colorado in autumn. For me, I feel a calm so welcome after my busy summer that this season is my mental health elixir. I grab my gloves, my walking stick and my dog, Rowley, and I am happy.

it's in the DETAILS

Take a small book in your backpack. Collect the prettiest leaves on the path and slide them in the book between the pages. When you get back home, satisfy the creative child in you and iron the leaves between two sheets of waxed paper to save I did a long running roll and used a table runner for the season.

From the Journals...

"We got married on Saturday in the backyard of the Loft. The yellow aspen leaves and magnificent pine trees made for a wonderful setting. The daily visits from the elk and deer was magical and made it totally endearing to everyone who shared this special day with us."

Carve a Pumpkin

jack-o-lanterns

Just down our road from the inn is a magical Pumpkin Patch each year. The brilliant orange "sea" of pumpkins appears overnight and I know that the fall season is in full swing. I have my favorite pumpkins I search out; I love the twisted, long "fresh off the vine" stem and I imagine the character of the face yet to be carved. Be still my knives. Pick your perfect pumpkin out together and make a date to design, carve, light and then just stand back to admire your work.

Being creative together is very sexy!

it's in the DETAILS

Wait until dark to light the candle and sit back and toast your jack o'lantern creation with a traditional hot buttered rum or mulled cider.

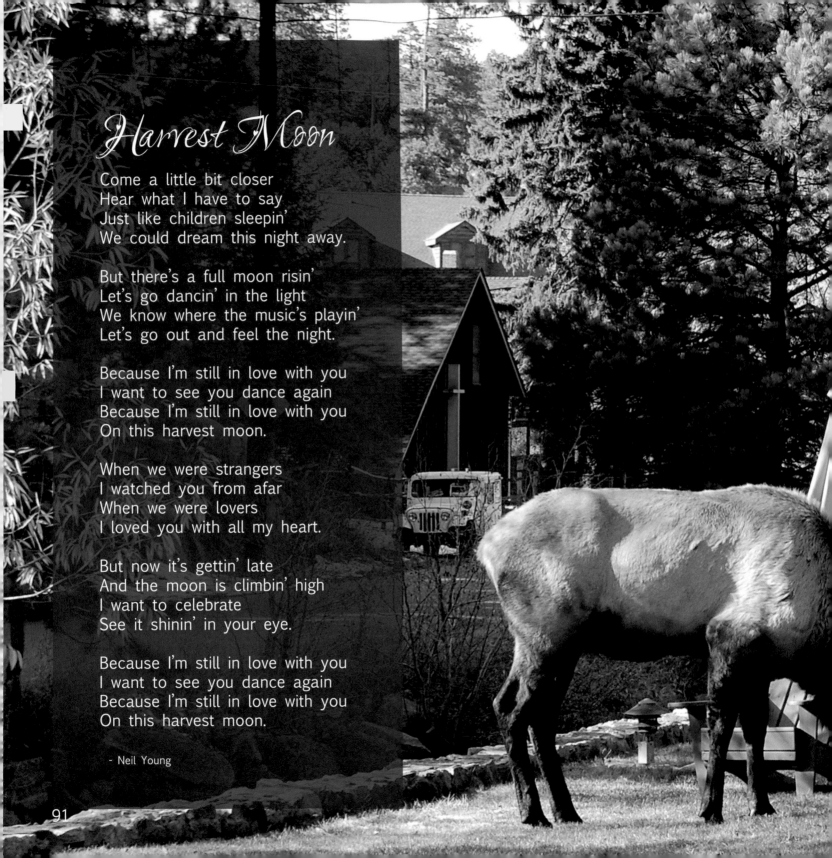

Harvest Moon

Come a little bit closer
Hear what I have to say
Just like children sleepin'
We could dream this night away.

But there's a full moon risin'
Let's go dancin' in the light
We know where the music's playin'
Let's go out and feel the night.

Because I'm still in love with you
I want to see you dance again
Because I'm still in love with you
On this harvest moon.

When we were strangers
I watched you from afar
When we were lovers
I loved you with all my heart.

But now it's gettin' late
And the moon is climbin' high
I want to celebrate
See it shinin' in your eye.

Because I'm still in love with you
I want to see you dance again
Because I'm still in love with you
On this harvest moon.

- Neil Young

Harvest Moon Dinner

bounties of autumn

Harvest Moon is the September full moon, traditionally associated with the fall bounty. This is when the leaves change color and temperatures fall and taste buds invariably start to crave fall-specific foods and flavors.

Just look to the freshest fall ingredients for a perfect fall dinner for two. Start with two chubby little Cornish game hens olive oil rubbed with fresh savories of rosemary, fresh basil, and thyme. If not in your garden, grab at the market the autumn vegetables that will be your dinner jewels. Add your favorites - squash, zucchini, vine-ripened tomatoes, or sweet potatoes. Keep it simple and straightforward, no need to fuss too much here. A light oiled coating grilled, baked or all together in a small casserole.

it's in the DETAILS

Autumn desserts are plentiful with pecans, pumpkins and glorious apples.
I offer here two of my most favorite (and my husbands!) that are classics.
Plus, they will make your kitchen smell amazing!

Viva Glam Champagne

To champagne in flute add:
- ♥ a splash of raspberry liqueur
- ♥ Top with a floating fresh raspberry

From the Journals...

"Here we are again...enjoying Evergreen, enjoying Colorado and enjoying each other. Peaceful, serene, quiet, a great place to find your center, your faith, your trust."

Autumn Breakfast

tempt your partner with this perfect start to any fall day

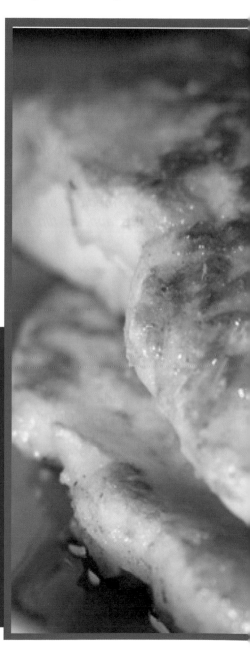

With cooler days and colorful trees in the anticipation of a slower paced season, take the time on a precious morning together to make breakfast out of the ordinary. Spice it up with this divine pumpkin latte to start. Share the newspaper over pancakes and sausage and savor your time...

it's in the D E T A I L S

Pumpkin Spice Latte

1-2 shots espresso (1/4 C. espresso or 1/2 C. strong brewed coffee)

1 c. half and half

1 T. canned pumpkin

Optional: pumpkin pie spice, nutmeg, or cinnamon.

In a small saucepan, stir pumpkin puree into half and half. Add the syrup. Heat on medium until steaming, stirring constantly. You do not want the milk to burn. In a blender on high speed add milk, use whip setting for 20 seconds until foaming. Pour the mixture into a tall glass and pour coffee over the top. Dust with ground pumpkin pie spice or nutmeg.

Trees of Love

Tree carvings fascinate me. I love discovering initials carved in a tree during a hike in the woods. I try to imagine the lovers that have made their mark. Was it a love they shared or perhaps a personal pining for someone not sharing the same feelings?

103

104

Winter

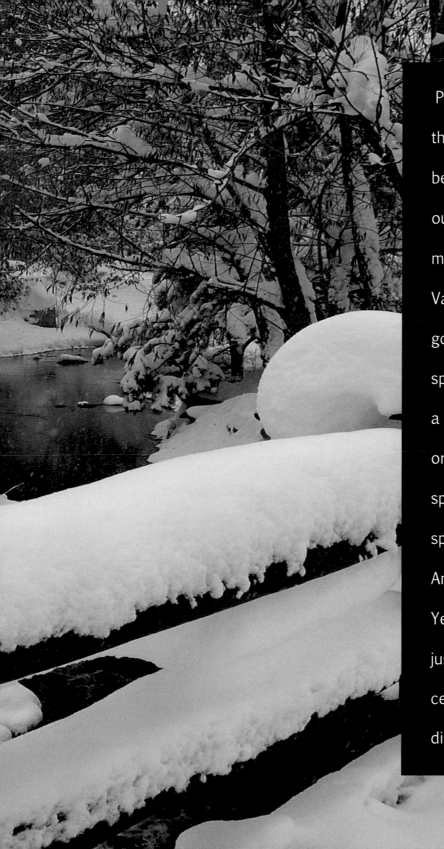

Perhaps the most romantic season of the four, winter brings a blanket of white beauty and chill and the celebrations our hearts embrace - Christmas/Christmas Eve, New Year's/New Year's Eve and Valentine's. As our trees and flowers go into dormancy and await the birth of spring, we can snuggle by the fire, make a snow angel or hike through the woods or parks. Preparing food has its own special appeal to make our celebrations special and unique for the one we love. And the libations flow in toasts of New Year, new love and new hope. Here is just what you need to help make your celebrations simple, meaningful and distinct.

From the Journals...

"I woke up before dawn to see a substantial snowfall. In the darkness, the fireplace came on and as I snuggled up to my husband, I was pretty sure I had died and gone to heaven."

"The way this place makes us feel is magical-we will always return."

Winter Outing

ice skating • snowshoeing • sledding • winter hiking

In Colorado, no matter the season, there is no better way to spend time with your love than outdoors. Winter is no different. With the season, the snow offers many activities that make for a great day together. In Evergreen, couples flock to the focal point of town, Evergreen Lake, for ice skating. Almost every town has an ice rink indoors or outdoors close by. If you are lucky to have enough snow on the ground and a meadow nearby - snowshoeing is as much fun. Is a snow-covered hill beckoning you to sled down it? You may decide to simply take a hike together. One of my personal favorites is to fill the yard with snow angels. No matter what you do, you will need proper nourishment and something to warm you up. This date will be simple: grab your thermos of hot chocolate, bake our favorite oatmeal raisin cookies, grab your mittens and scarf and you're out the door.

it's in the DETAILS

Shake up the hot chocolate a little and add peppermint, cinnamon schnapps, or your favorite flavored coffee creamer.
Don't forget to bring the handwarmers for your mittens - you can pick these up at almost any sports or outdoors shop and sometimes even at your local supermarket.

Got Mistletoe?

Just one kiss is all it takes,
To pledge a love to thee;

Under the mistletoe,
sharing bliss;
With a thank you kiss!

Just close your eyes.

115

Christmas Eve Dinner

a romantic holiday dinner for two

The gifts are wrapped and under the tree, your little ones may be tucked in or trying to get to sleep, so Christmas day comes faster. Or it is just you two and you are as excited as kids.

Now is the time, the quiet time, to enjoy a simple festive dinner for just you two. Set a spot with the best view in the house of your sparkly tree. Put on some holiday tunes to set the mood, grab a glass of wine to complement your soup. (Did you make in advance? Such a good idea!) Complete your meal with crusty bread and our perfect salad. For dessert look no farther than your kitchen counter for the holiday cookies and candies. Tonight you deserve a treat or two.

it's in the DETAILS

Stuff the stocking with a magical holiday getaway gift. It's something to look forward to and plan for. Fill the stocking with a brochure, a photo, a copy of a menu for a dinner celebration, a spa treatment gift certificate and, of course, a holiday love note.

Poinsettia Champagne

To each glass of champagne add...
- ♥ 1 teaspoon cranberry juice
- ♥ 1/2 teaspoon triple sec
- ♥ 2 cranberries to float in each glass

From the Journals...

"There is a place in ones heart that is 'home.' Much more than a destination, It is a feeling of safety. A warm blanket on a cold winter night. A candle in the darkness. A smile from a loved one when you felt so alone. My heart calls this place "home" and here as the sun streams through the towering pines, The water rolls and softly bathes the Mountain stones and as the breeze whispers softly of nature's magic. My soul is lifted My spirit is restored and I have, once again, come home."

Christmas Morning
a breakfast for two

The beauty of this date...no dressing up, nowhere to go - you're already there. Get up early enough to put together this simple and elegant breakfast. Serve it to him bedside if you don't mind crumbs in bed - or beckon him to a table set with everything he needs for a great Christmas Breakfast; piping hot coffee, a mimosa or bloody mary, steaming hot breakfast and you! The surprises are in the details - don't overlook these. If you can, start a Christmas tradition for just the two of you. Brew a pot of your most favorite java. I love to splurge on the Ghirardelli Chocolate blend.

it's in the DETAILS

I never tire of the sentiment in this little poem. It is a lovely way to set the tone of the most romantic winter holiday. Set a copy to read by your breakfast table. Start a tradition of your own with a favorite - maybe from one of your holiday cards. Seal it with a kiss and a tender embrace.

Christmas Prayer

May the spirit of giving / Go on through the year,
Bringing love, laughter / Hope, and good cheer.
Gifts wrapped with charity / Joy, peace, and grace.
Ribboned with happiness / A tender embrace.

"I drink champagne
when I'm happy and
when I'm sad.
Sometimes I drink it
when I'm alone.
When I have company
I consider it obligatory.
Otherwise, I never touch
it - unless
I'm thirsty.

-Madame Elizabeth Bollinger

125

New Years Eve

spend the night in together...and see where the new year takes you

At the inn, New Year's Eve and Valentine's Day top our most in demand nights. We turn away so many people as the demand is so big for a little bit of magic in the world of romance.

New Year's fills us all with the unknown and an unbridled optimism of a new start, a clean slate. And being with the one you love on New Year's Eve is our time to shine at the inn. We "put on the dog" with champagne trays of rich chocolates, beautiful flowers, poetry, and gifts. I start months ahead to top the year before, to impress and set the perfect moods.

In the morning we are ready with the most impressive breakfasts we can offer featuring my signature recipes from *Colorado Cravings*.

Have a look at the past year's favorites we offered. Easy to produce; hopefully here you will find inspiration!

it's in the DETAILS

The trick to opening a bottle of champagne while maintaining its integrity is to avoid "popping" the cork. Begin by scoring the foil around the base of the wire cage. Then, carefully untwist and loosen the bottom of the cage, but do not remove it. In one hand, enclose the cage and cork while holding the base of the champagne bottle with your other hand. Twist both ends in the opposite direction. As soon as you feel pressure forcing the cork out, try to push it back in while continuing to twist gently until the cork is released with a sigh.

R E C I P E S

1 clove garlic, halved
3/4 c beer
2 c shredded Swiss cheese
1 c shredded sharp cheddar cheese
1 T flour
dash hot sauce

Beer Cheese Fondue

Rub inside of pan with garlic. Add beer, heat slowly. Coat cheeses with flour and add to beer. Stir constantly until cheese is melted. Stir in hot sauce.

✧✧✧

20 milk chocolate or semi-sweet chocolate Hershey Kisses
2 T sugar
1 lg ctr. Cool Whip
1/3 cup milk
3 oz soft cream cheese
1 graham cracker crust (you can buy this)

Midnight Kiss Pie

Heat chocolate and 2 tablespoons milk over low heat, stirring until melted. Beat sugar into cream cheese; add remaining milk and chocolate mixture. Beat until smooth. Fold 3 1/2 cups of Cool Whip into chocolate mixture. Blend until smooth. Spoon mixture into crust. Top with remaining Cool Whip. Grate chocolate or make pretty curls to garnish. Freeze at least 4 hours. Remove from freezer about 15 minutes before serving.

JOURNALING

A resolution we would like to keep...

_____

_____

_____

_____

_____

_____

_____

_____

_____

_____

_____

_____

_____

_____

_____

_____

From the Journals...

"It was thirteen years ago today that I asked my wife to marry me in this very room. We are so glad to celebrate our 12th wedding anniversary in the very same room. We have stayed here many times and it just seems to get better year after year. Thanks so much for giving us a romantic place to reaffirm our vows of love!"

"To be 30 miles away from children, dogs, work...hardly seems possible. What an idyllic getaway, a special 12 hours. We'll be sure to return."

Movie Night

let the "Silver Screen" in your home spark your own love story

This night is great on the budget. Stay in and watch Silver Screen classics in your living room in your pj's. Surprise your love with a set of PJ's - even better share them. Give him the bottoms and you can wear the top. Get your favorite blanket and get ready to snuggle up and watch the movies he loves. What better way to your man's heart than with a Mile High Sub Sandwich, Root Beer Floats and homemade popcorn?

it's in the DETAILS

When a group of men were interviewd they admitted that they do in fact like "chick flicks." So don't feel compelled to look for a macho film to make him happy.

To My
Valentine

From the Journals...

'What a perfect place to spend Valentines Day. Last night my boyfriend asked me to marry him by the creek. It was truly amazing. There were loose petals in the snow and down to the table. On the table were candles, glasses of champagne and more petals. It was there he asked me to spend the rest of our lives together. It could not have been more perfect."

♥

'This beautiful, calm cottage is truly a magical getaway from the busy world! From the moment we arrived we didn't want to leave - every detail from the champagne chilled to perfection, to the wonderful chocolates created an atmosphere of serenity and relaxation. The morning arrived bright and sunny with a fresh covering of snow- how perfect. We are already planning our return. Thank you for a wonderful Valentines and Anniversary."

"Although this is our first week of marriage, this Valentines is already our second stay here. The rooms and the cottages here are among the most beautiful and cozy of any we have ever seen anywhere else. As if this is not enough we have been treated like old friends."

♥

"My husband and I have struggled through some very hard times in our marriage. Our relationship needed some TLC. He scheduled a surprise weekend away and didn't leave any hints as to where we were heading. Completely unaware of what he had booked for us (the Valentines Day Special) we arrived walked in and fell in love all over again. He took a chance and our stay has been unbelievable! The best part - we agree - is planning for our next trip back. Thank you for the romance, the ambience and the attention to detail. Two very re-connected people."

135

Valentines Day

i love you

This is a "Top 3" holiday for me. At the inn I begin planning months ahead for this holiday period. We attempt to "out do" the year before: an even better champagne tray offering, breakfasts designed to impress, the best romance quote, gift, décor, craft, confection, flowers and cookies. There is no end to the anticipation and excitement for me.

it's in the DETAILS

For this night - the details are in the music you choose to set the mood...Download these on your ipod and take them with you.

My Heart Will Go On - Celine Dion
Mr and Mrs. Jones - Al Green
Wonderful Tonight - Eric Clapton
No Ordinary Love - Sade
All for Love - Bryan Adams
Can't Help Falling in Love - Elvis
Crazy for You - Madonna
Have I told You Lately That I Love You - Rod Stewart
Kiss from a Rose - Seal

R E C I P E S

1 lb   macaroni
1 lb lobster meat
1 small onion
2 T unsalted butter
2 c milk
1 small clove garlic, minced
1 shallot, chopped
kosher salt and freshly ground black pepper
5 T flour,
5 T unsalted butter
2 T cornstarch and water
2 lbs grated cheese, mixture of gruyere, sharp cheddar & pecorino romano
3 T panko bread crumbs (Japanese)

Lobster Mac and Cheese

Cook the macaroni and set aside. Saute onion in butter. Add garlic and shallot and saute a minute longer. Add lobster meat, salt and pepper and milk and continue on very low heat. In another pot make a roux with remaining butter and flour. Mix together cornstarch and water in cup and add to roux, add lobster mixture and stir until hot. Add cheeses and stir until cheese melts and is creamy smooth. Add to macaroni and pour into well greased pan and top with bread crumbs and bake at 350 F for 20 minutes.

1/2 c brown sugar
1/4 c white sugar
2 T chili powder, paprika and garlic powder (of each)
1 t cayenne and dried mustard (of each)

Easy Dry Rub Steak

Mix together and apply a thick layer on each side of steak and grill to taste.

JOURNALING

He said "I love you" by...

_____

_____

_____

_____

_____

She said "I love you" by...

_____

_____

_____

_____

_____

_____

_____

_____

JOURNALING

JOURNALING

JOURNALING

JOURNALING

JOURNALING

....

JOURNALING

JOURNALING

....

_____

_____

_____

_____

_____

_____

_____

_____

_____

_____

_____

_____

_____

JOURNALING

_____
_____
_____
_____
_____
_____
_____
_____
_____
_____
_____
_____
_____
_____
_____

JOURNALING

_____

_____

_____

_____

_____

_____

_____

_____

_____

_____

_____

_____

_____

_____

_____

JOURNALING

· ·

_____

_____

_____

_____

_____

_____

_____

_____

_____

_____

_____

_____

_____

_____

_____

_____

_____

_____

JOURNALING